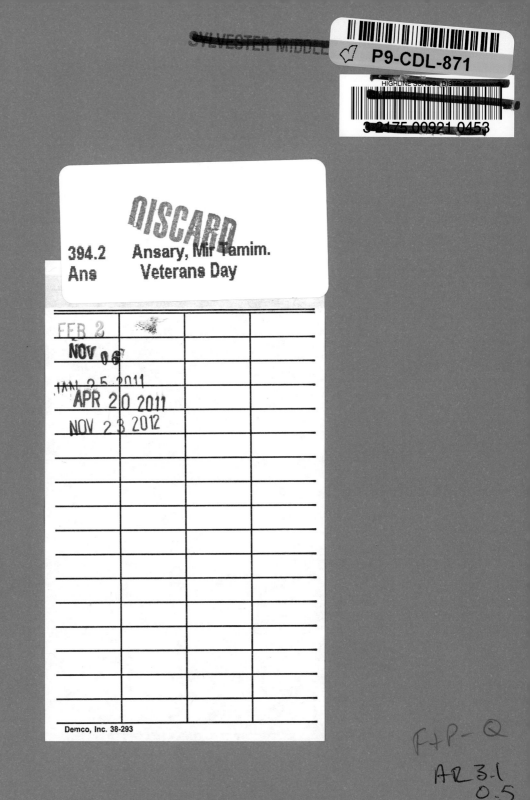

FEB 2

NOV 06

JAN 25 2011

APR 20 2011

NOV 28 2012

F+P-Q

AR 3.1
0.5

Holiday Histories

Veterans Day

Mir Tamim Ansary

Heinemann Library
Chicago, Illinois

Customer Service 888-454-2279
Visit our website at www.heinemannraintree.com

Designed by Kimberly Miracle and Q2A Creative
Printed in China by South China Printing Company

10 09 08 07 06
10 9 8 7 6 5 4 3 2 1

New edition ISBNs: 1-4034-8893-2 (hardcover)
                            1-4034-8906-8 (paperback)

The Library of Congress has cataloged the first edition as follows:
Ansary, Mir Tamim.
    Veterans Day / Mir Tamim Ansary.
        p. cm. -- (Holiday histories)
    Includes bibliographical references and index.
    Summary: Introduces Veterans Day, explaining the historical events behind it, how it became a holiday, and how it is observed.
    ISBN 1-57572-876-1 (lib. bdg.)
    1. Veterans Day – Juvenile literature. [1. Veterans Day. 2. Holidays.] I. Title. II. Series: Ansary, Mir Tamim. Holiday histories.

D671 .A75 1998
394.264 – dc21
                                    9814376

Acknowledgments
The author and publishers are grateful to the following for permission to reproduce photographs: AP/Wide World pp. 6, 7, 13 (all), 16, 18 (right), 19, 22, 26 (right), 28; Corbis pp. 12, 24-25 (Wally McNamee); Corbis-Bettmann pp. 8 (Alexander Alland Sr.), 18 (left), 20 (Baldwin H. Ward), 23; The Granger Collection pp. 9, 18 (center); Stock Boston p. 4 (Bob Daemmrick); UPI/Corbis-Bettmann pp. 10, 11, 14; SuperStock pp. 15 (all), 26 (left); Reuters/Corbis-Bettmann p. 27.

Cover photograph reproduced with permission of Alex Segre/Alamy.

Every effort has been made to contact copyright holders of any material reproduced in this book. Any omissions will be rectified in subsequent printings if notice is given to the publisher.

Disclaimer
All the Internet addresses (URLs) given in this book were valid at the time of going to press. However, due to the dynamic nature of the Internet, some addresses may have changed, or sites may have changed or ceased to exist since publication. While the author and publisher regret any inconvenience this may cause readers, no responsibility for any such changes can be accepted by either the author or the publisher.

Contents

Some words are shown in bold, **like this**. You can
find out what they mean by looking in the glossary.

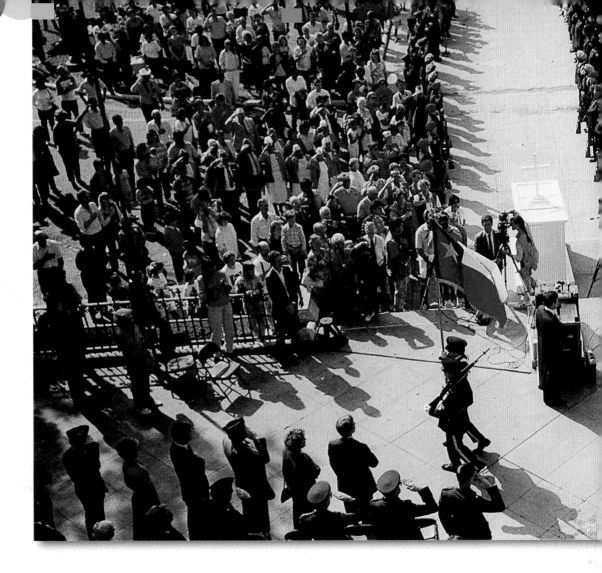

A Day for Veterans

November 11 is Veterans Day in the United States. A crowd has gathered in the park to watch a parade.

Many people think this is just another day off from school or work. But Veterans Day means much more to these people. That is because they are veterans themselves.

What Is a Veteran?

A veteran is someone who has been in the **armed forces**. Many of these veterans fought in wars. Some fought in the Persian Gulf War in 1991.

Some even fought in World War Two, way back in the 1940s. All these veterans risked their lives for our country.

Before Veterans Day

How did this holiday begin? Let's go back to a time before Veterans Day. Your great grandparents were young then. The United States was at peace.

But **Europe** was **tense**. In Europe, many small countries were ruled by bigger ones. Millions of angry people wanted to be free.

World War!

Some of the big countries wanted more land.
Their neighbors in other countries did as well.
Both sides were building strong armies.

In 1914 a war began. Germany helped one side.
Russia helped the other. Soon more than sixteen
countries were fighting.

The United States Fights

German submarines started sinking U.S. ships.
The United States decided to fight Germany.
In 1917 U.S. **troops** sailed to **Europe**.

The fighting stopped on November 11 at 11 o'clock, when Germany **surrendered**. World War One was over. More than fourteen million people had died.

Armistice Day

In 1919 President Woodrow Wilson called
November 11 a holiday. He called it Armistice
Day. Armistice means "to stop fighting."

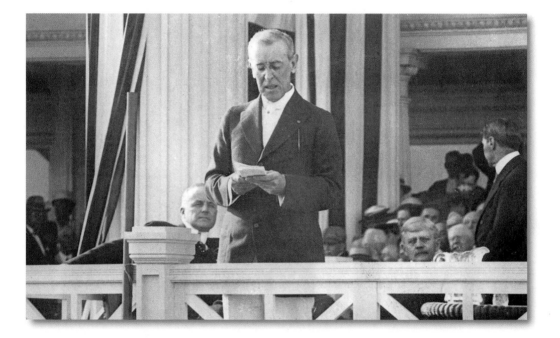

That day many people wore red poppies. They did so to remember Flanders Field. A bloody battle was fought in that poppy field.

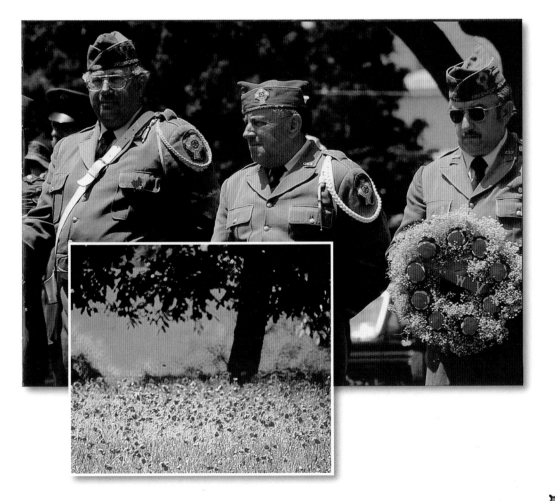

Honoring Peace

At eleven o'clock that day, many people became quiet. They kept silent for two minutes. This was a way to **honor** the peace.

These **customs** were repeated every year after that. People gave thanks for peace. They honored the soldiers who had won the peace.

German dictator
Adolf Hitler

Italian dictator
Benito Mussolini

Japanese general
Hideki Tojo

Trouble Again

But the peace did not last. Cruel **dictators** took over Germany and Italy. Powerful generals took over Japan.

These countries were called the Axis Powers.
In 1935 they started to attack other countries.
They planned to take over the world.

World War Two

The world fought back. In 1939 World War Two began. It was much more deadly than World War One. Armies now had more powerful guns.

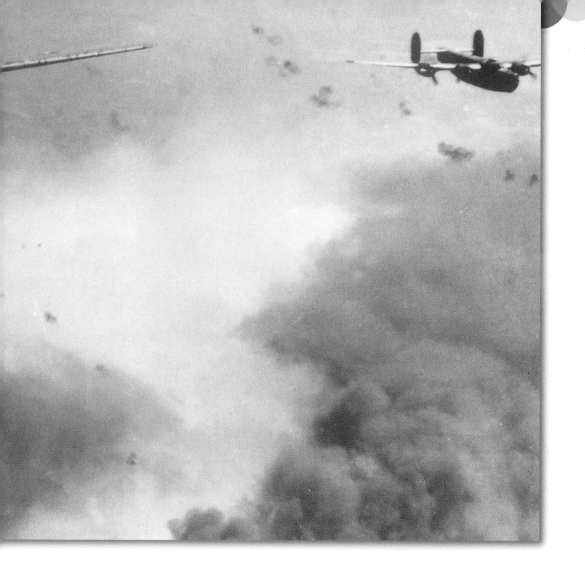

The war spread all over the world. There was
fighting in more than 50 countries. There were
battles on land, at sea, and in the air.

The Axis Powers Fail

In 1941 Japanese airplanes bombed U.S. ships and planes in Hawaii. After that, the United States entered the war.

The Axis Powers were **defeated** in 1945. World War Two ended. More than 50 million people had died in this war.

Celebrating Veterans Today

After the war, Americans were glad to celebrate Armistice Day again. In 1954 the name Armistice Day was changed to Veterans Day.

Now on Veterans Day, we celebrate all our veterans. Most of all, we **honor** those who died. We thank them for all that we have. They gave all they had.

Our Armed Forces

Today we have a powerful army, air force, and navy. We have the Marines and the Coast Guard.

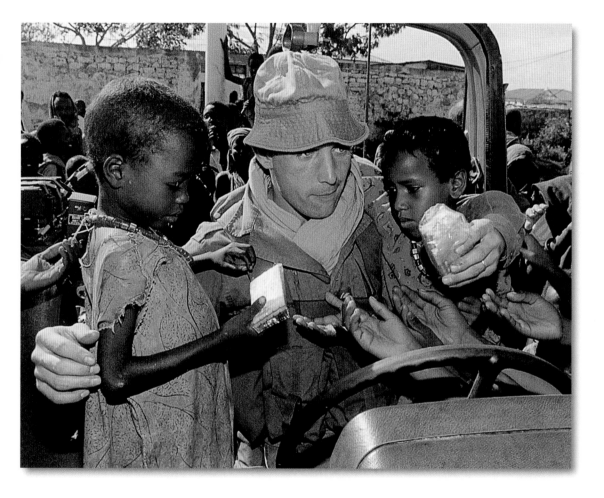

We stay ready even when there is no war. Our forces help keep peace in troubled places. We hope they can stop another war from starting.

The Eleventh Hour

The parade is over and the crowds are gone. But one veteran stays. This man loves peace because he has seen war. That is why he stands here on the eleventh day of the eleventh month.

The eleventh hour strikes at last. The veteran bows his head and falls silent. In his silence, he remembers friends who never came back from battle.

29

Important Dates

Veterans Day

1914   World War One begins

1914   The Battle of Flanders Field

1917   The United States enters the war

1918   World War One ends

1919   Armistice Day becomes a national holiday

1922   Mussolini takes power in Italy

1926   Army officers take power in Japan

1933   Hitler takes power in Germany

1939   World War Two begins

1941   Japan bombs U.S. ships at Pearl Harbor, in Hawaii

1945   World War Two ends

1954   Armistice Day is changed to Veterans Day

Glossary

armed forces country's army, air force, and navy

customs things people always do on special days or for certain events

defeated beaten

dictators leaders who use force to govern

Europe one of the seven continents

honor show respect for something

surrendered gave up

tense full of worry

troops soldiers

Find Out More

Landau, Elaine. *Veterans Day: Remembering Our War Heroes.* Berkeley Heights, NJ: Enslow, 2002.

Schaefer, Ted and Lola Schaefer. *The Vietnam Veterans Memorial.* Chicago: Heinemann Library, 2006.

Schuh, Mari C. *Veterans Day.* Mankato, Minn.: Capstone, 2003.

The Department of Veterans Affairs - Kids Page
http://www.va.gov/Kids/k-5/index.asp

Index